Contents

INTRODUCTION

Since their introduction to the Californian restaurant scene in the 1980s, microgreens have steadily gained popularity. These aromatic greens, also known as micro herbs or vegetable confetti, are rich in flavor and add a welcome splash of color to a variety of dishes.

Despite their small size, they pack a nutritional punch, often containing higher nutrient levels than more mature vegetable greens. This makes them a good addition to any diet.

Microgreens are little seedlings of edible plants that are often used to add color and flavor to meals. They're much smaller than regular greens, even "baby" greens, and have grown in popularity, especially in fine dining circles.

The term "microgreen" isn't specific to any one plant. Common microgreens include radish, cabbage, mustard, parsley, beet leaves, celery, and cilantro. Microgreens often have good nutrition—although people don't often eat them in large quantities, they're still high in vitamins and minerals. In fact, they have a much higher concentration of nutrients compared to fully mature plants.

CHAPTER ONE

What Are Microgreens?

Microgreens are young vegetable greens that are approximately 1–3 inches (2.5–7.5 cm) tall.

They have an aromatic flavor and concentrated nutrient content and come in a variety of colors and textures.

Microgreens are considered baby plants, falling somewhere between a sprout and baby green. That said, they shouldn't be confused with sprouts, which do not have leaves. Sprouts also have a much shorter growing cycle of 2–7 days, whereas microgreens are usually harvested 7–21 days after germination, once the plant's first true leaves have emerged.

Microgreens are more similar to baby greens in that only their stems and leaves are considered edible. However, unlike baby greens, they are much smaller in size and can be sold before being harvested.

This means that the plants can be bought whole and cut at home, keeping them alive until they are consumed. Microgreens are very convenient to grow, as they can be grown in a variety of locations, including outdoors, in greenhouses and even on your windowsill. Microgreens are young vegetable greens that fall somewhere between sprouts and baby leaf vegetables. They have an intense aromatic flavor and concentrated nutrient content and come in a variety of colors and textures.

Different Types of Microgreens

Microgreens can be grown from many different types of seeds. The most popular varieties are produced using seeds from the following plant families:

• Brassicaceae family: Cauliflower, broccoli, cabbage, watercress, radish and arugula

• Asteraceae family: Lettuce, endive, chicory and radicchio

• Apiaceae family: Dill, carrot, fennel and celery

• Amaryllidaceae family: Garlic, onion, leek

• Amaranthaceae family: Amaranth, quinoa swiss chard, beet and spinach

• Cucurbitaceae family: Melon, cucumber and squash

Cereals such as rice, oats, wheat, corn and barley, as well as legumes like chickpeas, beans and lentils, are also sometimes grown into microgreens.

Microgreens vary in taste, which can range from neutral to spicy, slightly sour or even bitter, depending on the variety. Generally speaking, their flavor is considered strong and concentrated. Microgreens can be grown from various seeds. Their taste can vary greatly depending on the variety.

Microgreens Are Nutritious

Microgreens are packed with nutrients. While their nutrient contents vary slightly, most varieties tend to be rich in potassium, iron, zinc, magnesium and copper.

Microgreens are also a great source of beneficial plant compounds like antioxidants. What's more, their nutrient content is concentrated, which means that they often contain higher vitamin, mineral and antioxidant levels than the same quantity of mature greens.

In fact, research comparing microgreens to more mature greens reports that nutrient levels in microgreens can be up to nine times higher than those found in mature greens.

Research also shows that they contain a wider variety of polyphenols and other antioxidants than their mature counterparts.

One study measured vitamin and antioxidant concentrations in 25 commercially available microgreens. These levels were then compared to levels recorded in the USDA National Nutrient Database for mature leaves.

Although vitamin and antioxidant levels varied, levels measured in microgreens were up to 40 times higher than those recorded for more mature leaves.

That said, not all studies report similar results.

For instance, one study compared nutrient levels in sprouts, microgreens and fully grown amaranth crops. It noted that the fully grown crops often contained as much, if not more, nutrients than the microgreens. Therefore, although microgreens generally appear to contain higher nutrient levels than more mature plants, this may vary based on the species at hand.

Microgreens are rich in nutrients. They often contain larger amounts of vitamins, minerals and antioxidants than their more mature counterparts.

Health Benefits of Microgreens

Eating vegetables is linked to a lower risk of many diseases. This is likely thanks to the high amounts of vitamins, minerals and beneficial plant compounds they contain.

Microgreens contain similar and often greater amounts of these nutrients than mature greens. As such, they may similarly reduce the risk of the following diseases:

• Heart disease: Microgreens are a rich source of polyphenols, a class of antioxidants linked to a lower risk of heart disease. Animal studies show that microgreens may lower triglyceride and "bad" LDL cholesterol levels.

• Alzheimer's disease: Antioxidant-rich foods, including those containing high amounts of polyphenols,may be linked to a lower risk of Alzheimer's disease.

• Diabetes: Antioxidants may help reduce the type of stress that can prevent sugar from properly entering cells. In lab studies, fenugreek microgreens appeared to enhance cellular sugar uptake by 25–44%.

• Certain cancers: Antioxidant-rich fruits and vegetables, especially those rich in polyphenols, may lower the risk of various types of cancer. Polyphenol-rich microgreens may be expected to have similar effects.

While this seems promising, note that the number of studies directly measuring the effect of microgreens on these medical conditions is limited, and none could be found in humans.

Therefore, more studies are needed before strong conclusions can be made.

Is Eating Them Risky?

Eating microgreens is generally considered safe. Nevertheless, one concern is the risk of food poisoning. However, the potential for bacteria growth is much smaller in microgreens than in sprouts.

Microgreens require slightly less warm and humid conditions than sprouts do, and only the leaf and stem, rather than the root and seed, are consumed.

That said, if you're planning on growing microgreens at home, it's important to buy seeds from a reputable company and choose growing mediums that are free of contamination with harmful bacteria such as Salmonella and E. coli.

The most common growing mediums are peat, perlite and vermiculite. Single-use growing mats produced specifically for growing microgreens are considered very sanitary. Microgreens are generally considered safe to eat. When growing them at home, pay special attention to the quality of the seeds and growing mediums used.

How to Include Microgreens in Your Diet

There are many ways to include microgreens in your diet. They can be incorporated into a variety of dishes, including sandwiches, wraps and salads.

Microgreens may also be blended into smoothies or juiced. Wheatgrass juice is a popular example of a juiced microgreen. Another option is to use them as garnishes on pizzas, soups, omelets, curries and other warm dishes. Microgreens may be eaten raw, juiced or blended and can be incorporated into a variety of cold and warm dishes.

How to Grow Your Own

Microgreens are easy and convenient to grow, as they don't require much equipment or time. They can be grown year-round, both indoor or outdoors.

Here's what you'll need:

• **Good-quality seeds.**

• A good growing medium, such as a container filled with potting soil or homemade compost. Alternatively, you can use a single-use growing mat specifically designed for growing microgreens.

• Proper lighting — either sunlight or ultraviolet lighting, ideally for 12–16 hours per day.

Instructions:

• Fill your container with soil, making sure you don't over-compress it, and water lightly.

• Sprinkle the seed of your choice on top of the soil as evenly as possible.

• Lightly mist your seeds with water and cover your container with a plastic lid.

• Check on your tray daily and mist water as needed to keep the seeds moist.

• A couple of days after the seeds have germinated, you may remove the plastic lid to expose them to light.

• Water once a day while your microgreens grow and gain color.

• After 7–10 days, your microgreens should be ready to harvest.

Microgreens can be conveniently grown at home. Those interested in harvesting their own microgreen crops can do so by following the simple steps above.

How Are Microgreens Grown?

Microgreen seeds are planted in flats or small pots and harvested two to four weeks later. They can be grown indoors or out. The little plants are ready to harvest as soon as they produce little true leaves. The microgreens are either pulled from the soil and rinsed or the stems are cut just above the soil. The plants are packaged and delivered to restaurants and a few specialty grocery stores.

You might be able to find microgreens at farmers' markets or some grocery stores, but they only last a week under the best of conditions, so they're not going to be shipped far and wide and you'll need to use them right away. Maybe a better solution is growing them at home?

Gardeners can easily grow microgreens right at home in their backyard or in a house, as long as there is a sunny window or lighting meant for growing plants. Microgreens don't take up much space and only require a couple of inches of potting soil. Plant the seeds a little more densely than you would for full-growing plants and mist the soil and microgreens regular to keep the soil damp.

Sprouts Are Not Microgreens

Edible sprouts, such as alfalfa sprouts and bean sprouts, have been around for a long time (although it's harder to find raw sprouts these days due to outbreaks of foodborne illness due to the consumption of uncooked sprouts). Microgreens and sprouts may look similar but there are some differences between the two.

One big difference is how they're grown. Microgreen seeds are planted and grown in soil, just like their grown-up garden counterparts. For sprouts, the seeds are germinated in water or wet bags for a couple of days, usually in warm dark places, until they sprout. At that point, they're ready to be packaged and shipped to stores.

The problem is that the growing conditions for sprouts increase the risk of bacterial contamination that causes foodborne illnesses. Since microgreens aren't grown the same way as sprouts, they don't have the same risk. Of course, they still need to be handled properly with food safety in mind, just like any raw veggie or green.

Another difference between the two is that when they're packaged, sprouts include the seed, roots, stems, and tiny undeveloped leaves. Microgreens aren't ready to harvest until they grow their first set of true leaves, and serving them with their roots is optional. It's usually easier to snip them off at the stem.

Microgreens Nutrition

In general, microgreens contain much higher concentrations of vitamins than fully grown versions of the same plants. One study examined 25 different varieties of microgreens and found that red cabbage had the most vitamin C, garnet amaranth had the most vitamin K1, and green daikon radish microgreens had the most vitamin D. In addition, the researchers discovered that cilantro microgreens had the highest concentration of two carotenoids called lutein and zeaxanthin.

Another study compared mineral content for fully grown green lettuce and lettuce microgreens and found the tiny greens had more calcium, magnesium, iron, zinc, and manganese than the fully mature plants.

Although more research is needed to know the full nutritional content of microgreens, a few brands are listed on the United States Department of Agriculture's Food Composition Databases. For example, one ounce of New Day Farms sunflower and basil microgreen mix has 25 calories, 2 grams protein, 4 grams carbohydrates, 2 grams fiber, 80 milligrams calcium, and almost 14 milligrams of iron.

Potential Health Benefits of Microgreens

There really isn't much research available for microgreens beyond the nutritional content, so it's hard to say for sure that eating any particular microgreen will produce any specific health benefits. While there are no studies that look at microgreen consumption in humans, one laboratory study found that overweight mice that were fed a high-fat diet and red cabbage microgreens had lower LDL-cholesterol (the bad kind) and didn't gain as much weight as mice fed high-fat diets alone or with mature red cabbage.

Of course, it's a long stretch from animal studies to humans, but it makes sense that microgreens from plants high in healthful phytochemicals, such as those found in red cabbage, could have similar health benefits. In fact, another study found microgreens from the Brassica species, including red cabbage, red mustard, purple mustard, and purple kohlrabi, actually have more complex and more varieties of polyphenols compared to mature plants.

How to Use Microgreens at Home

If you're lucky, you may be able to find microgreens in specialty grocery stores or farmers' markets. But be warned, they're probably quite expensive, right around 30 dollars a pound (makes that kitchen microgreen garden seem like a great idea). Some of the more common varieties include arugula, beet greens, basil, chard, carrot, cress, amaranth, spinach, and mustard. They have stronger flavors so only a little is needed to perk up your favorite dish. Choose microgreens that are fresh looking and store them in the refrigerator. Remember, they won't last long so use them up within a few days.

Microgreens can be used a number of different ways depending on the meal you are cooking. Use microgreens that have the colors and flavors that fit your taste buds. For example, arugula microgreens have a sharp pepper-like flavor. Beet microgreens have a bitter flavor but add a lovely reddish color to a dish. Carrot microgreens are slightly sweet and chard is both beautiful and has a milder flavor.

Add microgreens to a sandwich or wrap in place of regular lettuce. They can be used in place of, or in addition to, some of your favorite herbs, or you can make a salad with a cup or two of microgreens, some shredded carrots, chopped nuts, and a tangy vinaigrette. Microgreens can also be added to the top of a hot freshly baked pizza or roasted vegetables.

Microgreens Facts

Description

Microgreens (micro greens) are a tiny form of young edible greens produced from vegetable, herb or other plants. They range in size from 1″ to 1 ½″ long, including the stem and leaves. A Microgreen has a single central stem which has been cut just above the soil line during harvesting. It has two fully developed cotyledon leaves and usually one pair very small, partially developed true leaves. The typical stem and leaf configuration for micro greens is about 1" to 1½" in height, and ½" to 1"in width across the top. Microgreens can have surprisingly intense flavors considering their small size though not as strong as mature greens and herbs.

Microgreens are used as a fresh flavor ingredient primarily in restaurants serving upscale cuisine. These restaurants place a strong emphasis on both the creative presentation and flavor of their dishes. Microgreens' delicate, fresh appearance adds beauty and dimension combined with a range of distinct flavor elements

Microgreens have been popular in upscale culinary establishments for twenty years. Microgreens have become a solid ingredient in the finest restaurants, and Fresh Origins has grown from a tiny start-up to America's leading producer. Fresh Origins prides itself on providing the most consistent quality and wide variety available anywhere. In addition, we regularly introduce new and exciting Microgreen varieties to the culinary world.

History

Microgreens have been produced in the United States since about the mid 1990's beginning in Southern California, then San Francisco and spreading eastward after that. Initially, there were very few varieties offered. The basic varieties are Arugula, Basil, Beets, Kale, Cilantro and a mixture called Rainbow Mix. They are now being grown in most areas of the country with an increasing number of varieties being produced. Although many people who are learning about Microgreens for the first time assume they are used in salads, they are almost never used that way in fine-dining restaurants.

Living Microgreens

A form of Microgreens sold in a specialized growing medium, cellulose (paper) pulp, has been produced in Europe since about 2002. Recently, living Microgreens have been offered for sale in the United States as well. There are a few reasons why this format has not been widely utilized. This method requires more packaging in terms of either boxing or heavy plastic trays and growing medium resulting in a much higher cost for a significantly smaller yield. The quality is often soft and very stringy with this method. It is also more costly to deliver in this form. For those who care about sustainability, living Microgreens are the least sustainable and the most wasteful of our resources.

The other challenge with living Microgreens is that the product, may start out fresh and vibrant just as it is removed from the specialized growing conditions of a greenhouse, but once they are put in a restaurant kitchen or restaurant cooler, the quality and flavor quickly declines. While they can still be considered alive and growing, once removed from the greenhouse, they rapidly begin to get even more soft, stretched, and stemmy as they lose color and flavor.

Microgreens versus Sprouts

Microgreens are not the same as sprouts. Some articles about Microgreens characterize them as being very much the same as sprouts. There are several important differences. Understanding the different production methods of each can help clear up any confusion between them.

Sprouts are simply germinated seeds. What is eaten consists of the seed, root, stem and pale, underdeveloped leaves. The FDA seeks to regulate all businesses that produce sprouts due to numerous outbreaks of food poisoning (11 recalls/alerts in the past year alone). In 2011, 52 people died and thousands got sick from consuming organic sprouts in Europe. The European Food Safety Authority (EFSA) has now warned consumers against eating sprouts or sprouted seeds unless they are thoroughly cooked. Salmonella and Escherichia coli O157: H7 have been the major causes of sprout-associated illness outbreaks. Commercial sprout processors must follow rigorous FDA Guidelines for the production that include multiple laboratory tests of each batch for the presence of pathogenic bacteria, to minimize the threat of foodborne illness. Despite rigorous efforts to reduce foodborne illness caused by sprouts, more and more restaurants are no longer able to cope with the risk and have removed sprouts from their menus. In October 2012 one of the nation's leading food retailers; Kroger announced that it would no longer sell sprouts in its supermarket chains because of the potential for foodborne illness. "Sprouts are unavoidably unsafe products" said Caroline Smith DeWaal, Food Safety Director of the Center for Science in the Public Interest. Walmart Stores discontinued selling sprouts in 2010.

Sprouts are produced entirely in water. The seed is not actually planted. A high density of seed is placed inside of sprouting equipment or enclosed containers. The seed germinates rapidly due to the high moisture and humidity levels maintained in the enclosures. Seeds can also be sprouted in cloth bags that are repeatedly soaked in water. For most sprouts, the seeds are soaked and placed in a rotating drum or container, kept at or near 100% humidity and maintained at a temperature of about 80 degrees F. When this processing is finished, usually after about 48 hours, the sprouts are ready for packaging and sale. The sprouting process occurs in dark or very low light conditions. These dark, warm, wet, crowded conditions are ideal for the rapid proliferation of dangerous pathogenic bacteria.

After this process of soaking and repeated rinsing (2-6 or more times per day to prevent spoilage), the sprouted seeds are ready for consumption. This is long before the expansion of any leaves. These sprouted seeds are generally sold as a tangled mass of very pale roots, stems, and leaf buds. Properly grown Microgreens cannot be produced using these methods.

Microgreens are not processed in the water. Microgreen seeds are planted and grown in soil or a soil substitute such as peat moss or other fibrous materials. They are ideally grown in bright natural sunshine, with low humidity and natural fresh air. The seed density is a fraction of what is used in sprout processing so each individual plant has space in which to grow and develop. Most varieties require 1-2 weeks growing time, some 4-6 weeks. After the leaves are fully expanded the Microgreens are ready for harvest. They are cut above the soil surface and packed without any roots. Some Microgreens are sold while still growing, rooted in the soil or another growing medium so that they can be cut by the end user. The living trays are more expensive and lower quality than well-grown pre-cut Microgreens

If the stem is cut leaving root behind, and it is not produced in water, it is a Microgreen, not a sprout. Microgreens that are grown in sunlight with plenty of space and good natural air circulation have increased vigor resulting in more color and flavor with better shelf-life, compared to those grown under unnatural artificial lights.

The conditions that are ideal for growing Microgreens do not encourage the growth of dangerous pathogens. These growing methods would not work for the production of sprouts.

Various Microgreens Ready For Harvest

To minimize confusion, it is important to avoid using words like "sprouting" or "sprouts" when writing about or describing Microgreens. FDA inspectors do not always understand the differences, potentially putting a Microgreen grower in the position of explaining them or being shut down. There could be confusion if the grower has described Microgreens as being in any way similar to sprouts. The FDA will consider enforcement actions against any party growing sprouts commercially, who does not have effective preventive controls in place, involving extensive microbial testing and FDA oversight.

The potential for food safety issues with Microgreens may be increasing due to the number of industrial, vertical Microgreen operations in which low light intensity, low air circulation or most commonly, a lack of GAP (good agricultural practices) and GMP (good manufacturing practices) based food safety procedures. Certain provisions of the FDA's Guidance for Industry: Reducing Microbial Food Safety Hazards For Sprouted Seeds may be beneficial and prudent for growers of Microgreens to follow.

MicroGreens have much stronger, more developed flavors than sprouts making them an ideal flavor component with a broad range of leaf shapes, textures and colors.

General Specifications of a Microgreen

A Microgreen is a seedling having a a central stem which has been cut just above the soil line during harvesting. It has two fully developed cotyledon leaves, and usually one pair very small, partially developed true leaves. Differences in the size and leaf configuration are based upon the specific plant variety. For example, Micro Borage is a very large Microgreen. At 1″ in height, it has a pair of very large cotyledon leaves and no true leaves. By comparison, Micro Mint has extremely tiny cotyledon leaves and will have 3-4 sets of true leaves at about 1″ in height. More typical in size and leaf configuration for micro greens is Micro Basil at about 1-1 1/2″ in height, and 1/2″ to 1″ in width across the top and includes the cotyledon leaves and one set of very small true leaves.

Microgreens and Nutrition

In 2012, USDA researchers at Beltsville Maryland in association with the University of Maryland conducted a study on the nutritional properties of Microgreens. This study has been cited at least 13,000 times on the internet since then.

While the results seem promising, there are some concerns with the study. The primary issue is that they did not do the analysis of the mature versions used for the comparisons with the Microgreens. This comparison, of course, is the whole basis for making the claim that the Microgreens are more nutritious than the mature versions. Instead, they relied upon data from the analysis done by others probably a very long time ago, so it is unknown if the same methods of analysis were done.

Another concern: some of the comparisons were not correct such as comparing one type of amaranth in the micro form to a completly different type (and color) in the mature form or comparing a Micro Radish top to a mature Radish Root. In addition, some of the items tested were not actually Microgreens, but shoots. For future studies, there should first be a clear definition of what Microgreens are and the nutritional analysis should be done for both the Microgreen and the mature leaf, grown under the same conditions, in the same study using the same methods of analysis, rather than relying on outside data and variable varieties grown under different conditions to compare.

The takeaway from this study is indeed promising. The most important discovery in this study is that the researchers have found that the growing conditions can greatly influence the nutritional content of Microgreens. When grown in ideal conditions (bright natural sunlight) the nutritional content will be at maximum levels.

From the USDA 2012 study:

"It is also noted that golden pea tendrils, which are grown in the absence of light, processed much lower vitamin and carotenoid concentrations than pea tendrils grown under light, suggesting that light plays an important role on nutritional values during the growth of Microgreens."

If Microgreens are grown in homes on windowsills, or stacked on shelves in buildings, grown with artificial lights or even greenhouse grown in a less than ideal climate (cloudy or hot and humid), the resulting nutritional value will be vastly different (much less) than what was found in the study since those Microgreens were grown in natural sunlight in San Diego, California.

We are pleased to have worked with the USDA researchers on new studies in which the crops were properly grown, analyzed and compared. While the preliminary results have been mixed, there are positive health benefits being documented for publication.

Varieties of Microgreens

The seeds used to grow Microgreens are the same seeds that are used for full sized herbs, vegetables and greens. Microgreens are simply seedlings that are harvested before they develop into larger plants.

Commonly grown varieties of Microgreens include: Amaranth, Arugula, Beets, Basil, Cabbage, Celery, Chard, Chervil, Cilantro, Cress, Fennel, Kale, Mustard, Parsley, Radish, and Sorrel.

Several varieties can be mixed together to create combinations of tastes, textures and colors

CHAPTER TWO

Growing Microgreens

Materials

Growing microgreens requires only a few supplies. Some of these things you might already have around the house, while others will be just a minimal investment.

Trays

Due to the short period of time microgreens spend in their container, any shallow receptacle can be used to grow them. We find that standard 20 x 10-inch black plastic trays work well. These trays are often available at stores selling gardening supplies for around two dollars per tray. If you have a local nursery, you could check to see if they have any trays that would otherwise be thrown away. Especially in the spring, we have found that our local nursery gets small packs of annual flowers held in the same size trays and have no use for them. We have hundreds of trays that would have been an added investment if we hadn't found this niche. They are stackable, lightweight, reusable, and fairly durable.

Even when they start cracking they can be reused by stacking two together. Wood is another alternative.

If you feel inspired to make your containers out of wood, they would work just as well. You could even use an old baking pan; you would just need to cut a few holes in the bottom for drainage. What you are looking for is a shallow, lightweight, movable tray.

Another option is using a shallow flower pot. There are a few factors to be aware of when choosing a pot to grow your microgreens. Although easy to find, clay pots can hinder germination because of their tendency to dry out quickly and wick moisture from the soil. Choose a wide shallow pot over a large tall pot to maximize the surface area for your growing greens and minimize unnecessary extra soil use. You may want to use several pots as your yield will probably be less than if you were using a standard tray.

Whether you decide to use wood, plastic, or metal, proper drainage is very important. Although often overlooked, drainage is one of the keys for a plant to thrive. While being very important in the garden, it is even more important in your trays. If you are buying or collecting plastic trays, they will probably already have holes cut in the bottoms. If you are making your own trays, be sure to create slits or holes to allow excess water to flow through. If there is a lack of drainage, you will find stunted growth, rot, and mold in your greens.

The heart of any farm or garden is its soil, and microgreens are no exception. Choosing the proper soil to grow your microgreens in is vital. A rich, fertile soil is teeming with the biological and mineral interactions necessary for vibrant, nutrient-rich plants. Apart from a few elements acquired from the atmosphere, plants draw all of their nutrition from the soil and water.

During our first season of growing microgreens, we used several brands of potting soil, looking for the best. Throughout these trials we were astounded to see the differences between them. All of the soils that we used were labeled "organic" with ingredients such as earthworm castings, bat guano, compost, etc.

As our greens grew in these mediums, we quickly noticed dramatic differences in germination, growth, and overall health of the plants. Most of the cheaper soils touting the same ingredients fell short when it came to sustaining the dense growth of the greens.

The soil that stood out in both quality and performance had additional ingredients derived from the ocean such as kelp, crab meal, and shrimp meal.

While you could use a lesser-quality soil for other things, your microgreens will often demand more. Using a high-quality soil, you will enjoy strong, even growth and an increased yield. While yield per tray is less important for the home grower, a commercial grower must pay close attention to this detail. The cost of higher-quality soil is often absorbed by the yields you will reap from your trays. We suggest going to your local nursery or horticultural store and spending some time looking at the available options. Talk with the shop keepers and choose a few brands of potting soil to take home and experiment with. Make sure the bags are labeled with their ingredients so you know what you are getting.

Soil Press

After filling your trays with soil, you will need a tool to create a flat seed bed. When we first experimented with growing these greens, we cut a thick piece of cardboard in the shape of our trays. It worked well for the short term but in the long run became soggy and damaged from weather and wet trays. If sowing just a few trays at a time, cardboard is a good option, but you may need to replace it every once in a while. Cardboard is easy to find and is usually free.

As our operation grew, we needed a more permanent press. Instead of making another out of the same material, we found some wood scraps and constructed a press with a handle.

Quality seeds are another integral part of growing microgreens. Factors that will affect the viability of your seeds are storage, handling, age, and seed source. you sow one thousand seeds, the difference between a 95-percent germination rate and a 50-percent germination rate is quite noticeable. It can be disheartening to have gone through the effort of sowing and caring for your trays only to see a small percentage of your seeds come up.

When it comes to storing and handling your seeds, you will want to keep them cool and dry. Avoid great fluctuation in temperature and moisture. During hot, humid summer days, be mindful not to leave them in the sun or let them get caught in a summer thunderstorm. Properly caring for your seeds will maintain their viability for a longer period of time.

Your seed packets offer you valuable information such as germination rate, age, and seed variety. Unless kept in a special environment, your seeds will last two to five years depending on the vegetable. The amount of time that your seeds will stay viable is an average and depends on whether you keep them in proper conditions.

With access to the Internet, you have hundreds of seed companies at your fingertips. For the purpose of growing microgreens, you are looking for seed companies selling in bulk. Many companies will sell only small packets of seeds, which is what you would find at your local gardening store. When trying out a new company, start with a small quantity of seed. If requested, many companies will provide free samples. When you have found the varieties you like, you will probably want to move up to quarter-pound bags. If you notice yourself going through seed quickly, most companies offer price breaks at one and five pounds.

Due to the volume of seed you will be going through, price is a consideration. Obviously the commercial grower will go through quite a bit more seed than the home grower. Therefore, they might want to shop around to find the best combination of quality and price.

As you are browsing through seed catalogs, you will notice some companies offering both organic and nonorganic varieties. While we always advocate supporting small, local, and organic sources of seeds, they are not always available or affordable. Above anything is the importance of finding untreated seeds from reputable, service-oriented seed companies.

Something unique about growing microgreens is the need for seeds that not only have a high germination rate but also germinate at the same time. We have noticed with some of our seed stock what we call "wave germination." With these seeds there is a difference in the timing of germination within the same sowing. We have noticed as much as two to three days between the first and last seeds germinating. This phenomenon would usually go unnoticed by most people growing full-sized vegetables. However, since we are harvesting our greens just one to two weeks after germination, we need all of our seeds to "pop" at the same time.

Seed quality also plays a role after your seeds have come up. We have grown broccoli that had great germination but had terrible-looking cotyledons. We have had China Rose radish, which is normally a beautiful pink-stemmed microgreen, come up with white stems. We have also had purple cabbage range from dark purple to green. Some of these variations won't bother the home grower, but for the commercial grower these deviations can be frustrating.

Towels

Using cloth or paper towels is a quick and effective alternative to covering your seeds with soil. Usually one would cover a sown tray with a dusting of soil, enough to cover the seeds.

For the home grower, with access to a washing machine, cloth towels work well. We recommend a thin, lightweight cotton cloth. You will want to wash them frequently, as wet towels can build up mold and bacteria. In our commercial operation, paper towels have been extremely effective. With the amount of trays that we sow every week, using paper towels became a better alternative.

Between composting and using them in our vermiculture bins, paper towels fit easily into our system. Just remember to purchase unbleached natural paper towels, as you don't want to be watering bleach and other chemicals onto your germinating seeds and soil. Whichever type of towel you use, its purpose will be to provide a covering layer to keep your seeds warm and moist until they germinate.

Watering: Hoses, Sprayers, and Watering Cans

If you have a small garden or houseplants, you may already have some of the supplies you'll need to water your greens. If you are growing outside, a garden hose and a sprayer with several settings will be important. Make sure you can adjust the strength of its spray. Out of all the settings provided on our sprayer, a medium shower has been the most effective. If you are going to be growing indoors, you'll need a watering can. Make sure it has an attachment that allows the water to sprinkle out rather than pour out in one stream.

Since you are growing the greens so densely, air circulation is very important. You don't want to water them so hard that they fall and mat. If this happens, the lack of air and excess water will cause them to rot. If you find that your greens have fallen, you can try gently brushing them upright with your hand, or in other words, "fluff" them. The key to good watering is to be gentle yet thorough.

The pH Meter

The measurement of acidity or alkalinity of a solution is pH. A pH meter is an important investment when growing microgreens. The pH of your water will determine how well your greens are able to access the nutrients in the soil. If the pH is too low or high, these nutrients get locked up and become unavailable to the plants. Meters range in price from eight to eighty dollars. Cheaper options rely on liquid solutions and color matching while the more expensive meters are often digital and can be placed directly in the water being tested. We cannot say enough about the importance of testing the pH of your water. We spent our first two seasons unaware of the specific water pH needs of many of our crops. We struggled with some crops such as beet, basil, and amaranth, uncertain of what was causing the inconsistencies we were encountering. We came across rot and poor growth in many of our trays and spent a lot of time changing different variables in our system so that we could correct these problems. Nothing seemed to help permanently. We would often see promising results, only to find that the same problems came back in future sowings. While buying soil at our local horticultural store, we spoke with the owner about our plight. He suggested testing and monitoring the pH of our water. We found out that our water was very alkaline, registering at an 8 on the meter. While some of our Asian greens have been able to tolerate this high pH, we discovered that the crops that we had been having trouble with preferred a much lower reading. Once we adjusted according to their needs, all rot, damping off, and poor growth ceased. It was like magic. Still, we are astounded at the difference balancing our pH has made for our greens.

Adjusting the pH requires playing a little with chemistry. There are several different organic products available for lowering or raising pH. A simple solution for lowering pH (increasing your water's acidity) is using a bit of lemon juice.

Baking soda, powdered oyster shells, or powdered dolomite lime will raise your pH (increasing your water's alkalinity).

As we said earlier, once the pH is brought into the proper range for the crop, the plant is able to draw key nutrients from the soil. Now that we have begun taking care of this factor, we are able to grow our greens well into their true leaf stage.

Instead of becoming stressed and stunted, the greens have come to a new level of beauty. Although it may seem like another step, we believe that monitoring your pH is well worth it and can give you impressive results. Crops sensitive to high pH are noted in the Individual Crops chapter.

Lids for Germination

If you do not have a greenhouse to grow in, you will need to invest in or invent lids to cover your trays. This creates a "mini greenhouse effect" and keeps temperature and moisture at a more consistent state than if your germinating seeds were exposed to open air. This is especially important in dry climates or in seasons when there is larger fluctuation between the night and day temperatures.

If lids are not used, you may find your seed germination is greatly reduced, uneven, and much slower than covered trays. The extra expense is well worth it in order to get a good yield.

If purchasing your lids, any local horticultural supply store or nursery should carry them. If they are not available in your area, you can find them online.

Refer to the resource section of this book for specific Web sites. The average price seems to be around three dollars. Remember that you will want a lid that fits your container. One good thing about using a standard-size tray is that it is easy to find lids that will fit them. Keep this in mind if you decide to build your own trays or are using a flower pot. If you use a tray that is a different shape or size, you will need to create an alternative lid. For this you could use plastic bags or a pane of glass. If plastic lids are used, make sure they are stored in the shade to prevent melting and disfiguration of the plastic. If a pane of glass is used, keep the trays out of direct sun to avoid excess heat.

Heat Mats

Heat mats can provide extra warmth for warm-weather crops (such as amaranth or basil) or jump-start the germinating process of any seed. They are often unnecessary but can be especially helpful for starting seeds in colder climates.

Relatively inexpensive, heat mats can be found at local horticultural stores or online, ranging in size and price. Heat mats are powered by electricity and gently warm the soil from below.

Scissors for Harvesting

We find that scissors are the most effective tool for harvesting microgreens. Buying a separate pair solely for the use of harvesting is not a bad idea—that way they stay sharp and clean and make cutting easy. Having a couple of different sizes of scissors can be helpful for cutting different varieties and densities of greens as well. The most important thing here is sharpness. Once your scissors begin to dull, you can either buy a new pair or sharpen your existing pair.

After years of trying different sharpeners for our knives and scissors, we have recently found one that is highly effective. The difficulty with most manual sharpeners is keeping the bevel at a consistent angle while you sharpen. If you do not keep the angle of the bevel consistent, it becomes more and more difficult over time to maintain a razor-sharp blade. The sharpener we have recently found clamps to the back of any size knife or scissor blade and will allow you to sharpen it at a constant angle. This takes any guesswork out of keeping your blade sharp. For more information on how to find a sharpener, take a look at the

Making a clean cut through the stem is one important component to the longevity of your greens. The less cell damage done during the harvest, the longer they will hold. Once scissors are allowed to dull, they will start to tear the stems of the greens versus making a clean cut. If stored for later use, you may notice deterioration and discoloration at the bottom of the stem where they have been poorly cut.

Scale

A scale is essential only for those planning to sell their greens. You will find many options available online or at local restaurant supply stores. They will range in price from forty to four hundred dollars. When choosing your scale, precision is the most important factor. As you will be dealing in ounces and fractions of ounces, you will want to find a scale that will give you a reading of 1/10-ounce increments.

Any small standard house fan with a few settings to choose from will work well for drying greens you plan to store or sell. You will want to choose one that either rests on the ground or has a pivoting head so that it can be pointed directly on your drying greens. We recommend a low to medium setting that won't overdry your delicate microgreens.

Storage Containers

You have a few options for storing your harvested greens. If you are planning to sell your greens to others, you can use either food-grade resealable bags or plastic clamshells. Both of these are available in bulk from various suppliers. For greens grown for home use, any bag or sealable container will work. Treat your microgreens as you would any delicate salad green.

How-to-Grow Ten-Step Process

Growing microgreens is a simple process that can be done in ten steps. You will discover that it takes little time, energy, and experience. You will quickly become skilled and efficient as you integrate the growing of fresh, nutritious greens into your life.

Step 1: Filling Your Trays with Soil

Now you are ready to grow microgreens! The first step is to fill your trays with the growing medium that you have chosen, creating the seed bed. We find that filling the trays with about an inch to an inch and a half of soil is sufficient. Use your hand to level out the soil. Make sure not to fill your trays to the very top to avoid soil and seed spilling over the edges when you first water. Use your soil press to smooth and flatten the soil, being mindful not to compact your seed bed.

Over compaction will result in poor, slow growth.

Step 2: Sowing Your Seeds

Now that you have a smooth, even seed bed, you are ready to sow your seeds.

Take a small pinch of seeds with your fingertips and sprinkle them over your tray using the same motion as if you were spicing a dish in the kitchen. Take your time to evenly spread the seeds over the entire tray. If you find that you have sown too many or too few seeds in any portion of the tray, simply add more seed or spread out the excess. You can either stick to one variety for your entire tray or sow as many types of seed as you like, creating a mixed tray. This is nice if you are sowing only a couple trays at a time but still would like a variety of greens to eat. The only thing to be aware of when growing a mixed tray is to use varieties that are able to be harvested at approximately the same time.

The density of sowing depends on the seed variety and the size at which you would like to harvest. If you want a dense tray of cotyledons, we recommend broadcasting a thick layer of seed.

If you would like to experiment with growing your greens to their "true leaf" stage, simply sow them less densely and allow them to grow for a longer period of time. In the beginning, it may take some experimenting to get your sowing down. You may find that you have sown some varieties too densely and are encountering poor growth and rot in your trays. On the other extreme, if you have sown them too sparsely, your yield per tray will be very low. Soil quality also plays a role in sustaining the growth of your greens. Start out with just a few trays and find your balance. Once your tray has been sown, you will want to give it a light pressing. The objective is to very lightly seat your seed in the soil, again being mindful not to compact it. Seating your seed ensures that your seeds have contact with the soil so that they can easily set roots.

Step 3: Covering Your Seeds

For this step you have three options. Traditionally, one would cover his or her seeds with soil; a layer about the depth of whichever seed is being sown, but making sure the seed is covered. Another option is to cover with cloth or paper towels. Your third option is to leave your seeds uncovered if you are germinating them in a dark place. Out of these three methods, we believe covering trays with towels to be the easiest and most effective.

Covering with Soil

If you to choose to cover with soil, smaller seeds (i.e., brassicas, endive, amaranth, etc.) will require you to cover them with sifted soil. While soil sifters are available, we find that using a pasta strainer works just as well and can be found in most kitchens. Simply put a handful of soil in the strainer and shake it over your trays. After doing this you will be left with the larger pieces of your potting soil that won't fit through your strainer. Set these aside and repeat this step until your seeds are covered. When covering your larger seeds (i.e., pea, chard, beet, etc.), sifting is unnecessary. Just take a handful of soil and sprinkle an even layer over the tray. After you have covered your tray, you will want to give it another gentle pressing. Apply the same amount of pressure as when seating your seed. If you find that once you have watered your trays you are starting to see seeds on the surface, just sprinkle a little more soil over the top.

Covering with Towels

An alternative to covering with soil is to use cloth or paper towels. While we don't use this method for most large seeds, it is extremely effective for covering smaller seeds. Laying a towel over your sown trays creates a moisture blanket.

Take your lightweight cotton or paper towel and lay it directly on your seeds.

Once in place, keep moist until the seeds have germinated.

After our first season, we started experimenting with towels. We found that the towels had all the benefits of covering with soil and none of the drawbacks. This method started saving us time and money. We cut our soil costs and saved time covering our trays. Towels also allow you to sneak a peek into the day-to-day progress of your germinating seeds. This can be entertaining to children, as they can look under the towel and watch the seeds slowly open and develop into plants.

With this method you are not covering the seeds with anything. This means more time must be spent monitoring moisture to ensure germination. Your trays will need to be under some kind of protection, whether it be a greenhouse or lids. It will also be helpful to keep these trays out of direct sunlight, especially in the summer. This will help with maintaining adequate moisture. If you choose to leave the seeds uncovered, pay careful attention when seating them.

Step 4: Initial Watering

The next step is to water your trays. Set your sprayer to a light/medium shower setting so that the entire tray gets gently soaked. Preliminary watering is the only stage at which overwatering is not an issue as long as your seeds are not drowning in water. However, underwatering will result in poor or no germination. A germinating seed must remain moist. If the seed bed, and therefore the seed, is allowed to dry out, the process will halt and your seeds will no longer be viable.

Step 5: Cover with Lids

Once your trays have been watered, you will need to cover them with lids if you are not growing in a greenhouse of some sort. The reason for using these lids is to speed up germination by holding in heat and retaining moisture. Keep in mind that if using plastic lids, you will want to keep a close eye on your trays when in direct sunlight. Due to the "mini greenhouse effect" that the lids create, temperatures inside can become substantially greater than the air outside. This is a benefit for stimulating germination and growth, but it must be monitored in order to avoid excess buildup of heat in your trays. If you notice that things are a bit too steamy inside, simply move the lid slightly to the side to create some ventilation.

Step 6: Watering Your Germinating Seeds

As your seeds are germinating, it is important to keep a close eye on their progress and to maintain proper moisture. When using the towel method, observe the dampness of the towel and water daily, keeping the towel and the seed below it moist. One benefit of the towel method is that it gives you a window into the germination process. Instead of the seeds being hidden from your view, you can lift a corner of the towel at any time, allowing you to watch the stages of germination. You want your seeds to remain covered until they are fully germinated. After a few days, you will notice that the towels will have started to lift off the soil, giving you a hint that your greens are getting ready to need to see the light. As illustrated in the photographs, certain germinating seeds acquire a white fuzz on their stems. This is not mold and is a natural part of the process as your seedlings set roots.

Trays covered with soil will require a bit more attention. Soil will dry out more quickly than towels, so make sure these trays are watered a couple of times a day. With microgreens, your trays will be so densely sown that when they germinate, the covering layer of soil will lift with the seeds. If the soil is not evenly rinsed from the seeds early in this process, they will remain under the soil in darkness. These seedlings will quickly become weedy and pale. When watered at this point, the covering soil can drown and kill much of the tray. That said, we covered our seeds with soil our entire first season of growing our greens. While it is not difficult to do, losing trays because you are a few hours off can be frustrating.

If you choose not to cover your seeds, take caution when watering. A gentle shower will ensure that your germinating seeds aren't disrupted. Remember that whichever covering method you choose, your seeds will need consistent moisture to germinate.

Step 7: Finding A Good Spot To Grow

One thing that makes growing microgreens so accessible to so many people is the lack of space they require. People often refer to us as "porch farmers," as we are able to support our entire microgreen client base on less than 100 square feet.

If you don't have enough room to plant a garden in the backyard or don't even have a backyard, a windowsill, porch, patio, or front step will provide plenty of space to grow fresh, delicious microgreens for yourself and your family.

As we all know, plants need light to thrive. The germination process, however, does not require light. This allows you to keep your germinating trays anywhere, so long as they are kept warm and moist. Once germinated, microgreens, like most other plants, require light to grow and flourish. This process of taking sunlight and converting it to energy is known as photosynthesis and is a fundamental process in the growth of your greens. Once your seeds have germinated, you will want to find a sunny spot inside or outside for them to grow.

Choosing the location of your trays requires paying attention to your greens. In the heat of the summer, some varieties may prefer full sun, while others require dappled shade. No matter what the variety, some amount of light and warmth are required. You will find that plants deprived of light will begin reaching for whatever light source they can find.

They will then become "leggy" and scrawny as opposed to being strong, stout healthy-looking plants. You will also notice a change in their color. While the trays given enough light are looking like a dense lawn of richly colored greens, the trays deprived of light will begin looking yellow and weak, making them more susceptible to rot and disease. This is easily avoided. Let them see the light! Strive to find a place for your greens that provides the most amount of sunlight. A sunny windowsill, your porch ledge, or even your front step could all serve as great places to grow your greens.

If you feel you are unable to get adequate sunlight, grow lights are also an option. There are a variety of grow lights available from your local gardening store or online, ranging in size and price. Keep in mind your energy costs when purchasing a system. Living in sunny places, you may never use them, but they could be quite helpful in places where sunlight is scarce during the winter months. Grow lights can be set up anywhere that is convenient. A basement or unused closet could easily be transformed into a greens-growing haven.

Step 8: Maintaining Your Growing Greens

Now that your seeds have germinated, they will require light to grow and thrive.

If you are using the towel method, you will now want to remove the towel and the plastic lid. Once the towel is removed, it can be composted, used in a vermiculture system, burned, or thrown away. If growing indoors, you can flip your lid over and place your tray inside. This will keep excess water off of your counters. Be sure to empty this water daily so that your soil isn't standing in water.

Depending on the variety, the greens will need to remain in the light for an average of seven to fourteen days. A fast-growing green like arugula will require a minimum growing period, while slow-growing basil will need more time.

Keep in mind that weather, location, and watering patterns all play a role in this timeline. While you may go through several growing cycles with the same results, great variation does tend to occur if any of the previously named factors are altered. Should you decide to branch out after experimenting with some basic varieties, you will notice that more exotic microgreens such as mint or sorrel will take substantially longer to both germinate and grow to size. Specific data on average germination and growth times for a number of crops is located in the Individual Crops chapter of this book.

Since your seedlings are now out in the light, you must pay attention to their moisture. Merely looking at the surface of the soil will not give you an accurate reading of its moisture content. You will need to get your hands dirty. Stick your finger in the corner of the tray to make sure that all of the soil is wet. Watering once a day is often sufficient—just be careful not to overwater. Overwatering at this stage can drown the seedlings and stop the growth process. Underwatering will result in wilted greens. Once their cellulose structure has been compromised by either over-or underwatering, the greens may remain damaged but are often able to recover. You might notice this if you have chosen a poorly lit place for your greens and later relocated them. You could also leave your greens during a cloudy day, thinking you have watered them sufficiently, only to find that it is sunny when you return and your greens have wilted. Often, a gentle soaking will revive them after a couple of hours.

This phenomenon occurs all the time in nature, especially in hot, dry climates where plants must preserve their energy. If facing intense direct sun and thereby heat, energy is sent to the roots to sustain the life of the plant, allowing the leaves and flowers to droop and wilt during the heat of the day. One could come upon such a plant midday and think it was dying, only to find the same plant in its full glory during the coolest part of the evening. That said, you want to avoid as much stress on your greens as possible, keeping them properly watered. Take note of the strength of the sun and avoid watering midday. When plants are watered in the heat of the day, the drops of water act as little magnifying glasses and can burn the leaves. This is easily avoided by watering either in the morning or evening in climates and times of year when the sun is at its strongest.

Step 9: Harvesting

Microgreens can be harvested at different stages of growth. You can either harvest them just after their cotyledons have opened or wait for them to put on a second set of leaves, known as true leaves. If allowed to continue to grow, eventually the greens will begin to show signs of stress such as yellowing, stunted growth, and looking weak or "leggy" (tall and unhealthy), and they will start to rot from underneath. This generally starts to happen because of how densely you are sowing the seeds and the small amount of soil you are growing them in. If the same seed were allowed to grow less densely, in a bigger container or directly in the ground with plenty of room for its roots, you could watch it grow through many stages. Depending on the variety, it would eventually grow into a full-sized plant from which you might harvest its fruit or leaf (i.e., a head of broccoli or full-grown leaves of arugula). Soil quality also plays a major role in the health and vitality of your greens. If you are using a lesser-quality soil, signs of stress will become apparent much earlier and more frequently.

How to Harvest

When getting ready to harvest your greens, one of the most important factors to be aware of is the heat of the day. Cutting the greens while they have been in the sun for a few hours or even in the shade during a hot summer's day will result in wilted greens that will quickly turn to mush. You can always try soaking them in cold water to revive them, but they are usually too far gone to perk back up.

Early mornings and evenings are the ideal times to harvest. The key here is to keep your greens cool. Harvesting at the proper time will keep them looking as fresh and alive as when they were growing. This is especially important for greens you plan to sell to others or store for yourself.

We find that scissors make the most effective tool for harvesting microgreens.

Think of cutting your tray like giving your greens a haircut. Hold a section loosely with one hand and use the other hand to snip with your scissors. Your greens may range from one to four inches tall, depending on the variety and age at which they are cut. To get a nice ratio of greens and stem, cut about one inch above the soil for most greens. If the greens have been allowed to get tall or you prefer less stem, cut higher up. After your cut, take the greens in one hand and loosely flick the stem side of the cut to knock off any soil or damaged ends. This step will keep your home salad clean and will save time washing if you are planning on selling your greens. After cutting, put each handful in a bowl or on a plate and use as much as you need. Unless you are cutting above the cotyledons, your trays will not grow again. The remaining soil and roots can be composted.

The chapter on composting will give you more information on "recycling" your used soil.

We harvest our greens differently if we are cutting to sell or if we are making a home salad. When harvesting for our restaurant orders, we use a small digital scale and zero out the weight of a plate to get accurate weights as we are cutting.

We usually harvest a bit more than we need to account for lost weight after washing. When we are harvesting for ourselves it's much more casual. Obviously we do not use a scale and often snip a bit from several trays, making a custom salad as we like it. Don't feel like you have to harvest a whole tray or harvest from only one variety at a time. You can also experiment with greens at different stages of growth and create a unique mix by using just a couple of varieties at different sizes. This will provide different textures and a varied look to your mix.

One of the greatest things we find about growing microgreens is the ability to cut and eat them within minutes. This allows you to have the freshest, tastiest, and most nutritious salad available right from your own home. In the Recipes: Food as Art chapter, we describe different mixes we like and pair them with recipes for you to explore, but keep in mind that your only limitations are your taste buds and imagination.

Step 10: Washing and Storage

Unless you are planning on selling your greens to restaurants or individuals, it is often unnecessary to wash them. You can treat them as you would salad greens from your garden or the store by giving them a quick rinse before serving them.

Some growers choose not to wash their greens before they sell them. In operations where soil-less methods are used (i.e., hydroponics), selling unwashed greens is more of an option. However, if growing with soil, washing the greens is important so that you can offer a clean product, free of soil and rotten leaves. The process of washing the greens gives you a closer look at your product and allows you to remove any soil, debris, seed hulls, or rotten leaves before you sell it to your client. This will give you the confidence of knowing exactly what you are selling as well as an edge over any competition selling unwashed greens.

The process of washing microgreens is simple but can also be tedious and time consuming. We find that purchasing a plastic tub to use solely for washing greens is convenient. You will want to find a size that fits in the sink where you will be washing to have easy access to running water. Wash your greens in cold water to maintain freshness. Proper lighting is important so that you can get a good look at your harvest and remove any duff or rotten leaves easily.

We find that a well-lit room and the use of a headlamp makes this process much easier.

Technique varies in the cleaning of greens. Most of the seed hulls, seeds, duff, and damaged leaves float to the top, where they can be easily skimmed off using your hand. Soil and other heavy particles often sink to the bottom. This process takes an eye for detail and a great deal of patience. In order to really showcase your greens, we find it important to be impeccable with your processing. While this may seem daunting at first, with practice, you will become both skilled and efficient. You may find that you invent new methods that help you to streamline processing. Different crops often call for different methods. While some greens are effortless to wash, others prove more difficult and require more time and attention. We have found that greens that are especially dirty or full of damaged leaves require a two-stage washing method. After the initial washing, we take out a handful at a time, examine it on a plate, pull out anything we have missed and continue until finished. Often, these greens will require a second rinse. If you choose to use the "towel method" for covering your germinating seeds, they will require far less washing than if covered with soil. Covering with towels eliminates half of the soil and seed hull normally found in your rinse water, thereby cutting your work in half. When we switched from covering with soil to covering with towels, we went from three to four rinses per crop down to one or two.

After your greens have been washed, your next step is drying. Using a small fan is very effective. You will want to use your fan on a low to medium setting and be sure to keep an eye on the greens. You will need to turn and fluff them every few minutes, being careful not to overdry them. Your beautiful, delicate microgreens can turn quite the opposite if allowed to become over-or underdried and stored in the refrigerator.

If you are storing your greens for yourself, we recommend using a resealable bag, filled with a bit of air, and putting it directly in the refrigerator. Another option is using a reusable container. Although quite perishable, microgreens will last at least three to four days and often up to a week or more, depending on their quality, variety, and the amount of moisture in the container.

If your greens are being sold, you will want to invest in a small accurate scale and either food-grade resealable plastic bags or plastic clamshells (resources available in the back of the book). We find selling four-ounce packages to be convenient for both the chef and the grower. Creating a label of some kind is useful to distinguish the date the greens were harvested as well as their variety.

CONCLUSION

Microgreens are flavorful and can easily be incorporated into your diet in a variety of ways. They're also generally very nutritious and may even reduce your risk of certain diseases. Given that they're easy to grow at home, they're an especially cost-effective way to boost nutrient intake without having to purchase large quantities of vegetables. As such, they're a worthwhile addition to your diet.

Serving microgreens alongside (or on top) of any dish is a great way to add a few more vitamins and minerals to your balanced diet. However, since they have so much flavor, only a small amount of microgreens are usually needed. A tiny microgreen salad may not replace a big healthy garden salad for fiber content and volume, but it still packs a nutritional punch